BLAST BACK!

WOMEN'S SUFFRAGE

by Nancy Ohlin   illustrated by Roger Simó

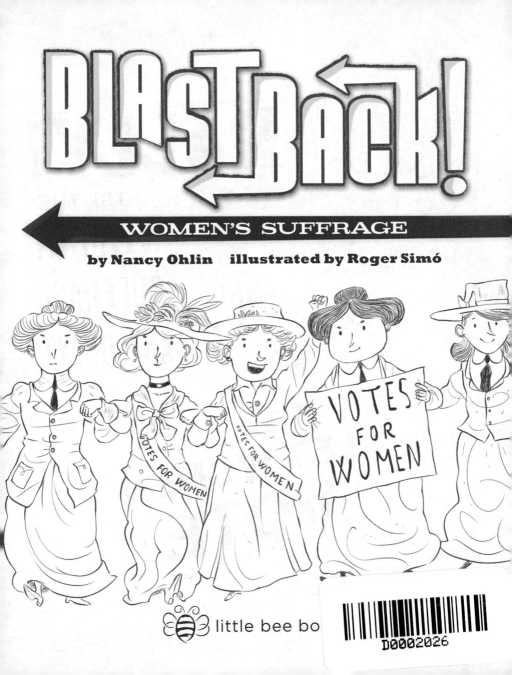

little bee bo

CONTENTS

Introduction

Have you ever heard people mention women's suffrage and wondered what they were talking about? What exactly does "suffrage" mean? And what does it have to do with women?

Let's blast back in time for a little adventure and find out. . . .

A Brief History of Women's Suffrage

Women's suffrage is the right for women to vote in political elections. Through political elections, people can vote for and help choose their leaders, such as presidents, prime ministers, governors, mayors, and national representatives, like senators, congressmen, congresswomen, and Members of Parliament. Through political elections, people can also vote for the addition of new laws or the repeal (or removal) of old laws.

For a long time, women around the world did not have the legal right to vote. The organized struggle for women's suffrage began in the nineteenth century in Great Britain, the United States, and some other places.

By the end of the twentieth century, women had gained the right to vote in many—but not all—countries.

Other terms for "women's suffrage" are "woman suffrage" and "women's franchise." "Franchise" is another word for "suffrage." The word "suffrage" comes from the Latin term *suffragium*, meaning "vote," "voting rights," and "ballot."

WOMEN
bring all
VOTERS
into the world
~
Let Women Vote

RALLY!
FOR THE
WOMAN
SUFFRAGE
AMENDMENT

LET WOMEN
VOTE

National Women Suffrage Association
1919

Why Is Women's Suffrage Important?

Throughout history, there has been inequality (or unequal treatment) in people's rights based on one's gender, race, ethnic background, sexual orientation, and other factors.

Women's right to vote is just one example of this inequality. Women have been denied the right to vote throughout much of history, dating all the way back to the ancient Greek and Roman civilizations. Some men have been denied as well— because of race, for example, or whether they owned property or were educated and/or literate (which means able to read and write).

When all of a country's citizens do not have a say in their government, power can fall into the hands of a few. This can result in an authoritarian and tyrannical government that doesn't always— or some would say ever—act in the best interests of its citizens. Examples of such governments are Germany under Adolph Hitler, South Africa when it practiced apartheid (which was an official policy

of discriminating against Black and mixed-raced people), and present-day North Korea.

Democracy is a form of government of the people, by the people, and for the people. The right to vote is a cornerstone, or one of the foundations, of democracy. If everyone doesn't get a right to vote, then only certain groups are represented and get a say in how everyone is governed.

A Woman's Place?

You might be wondering: Why were women denied the right to vote for so long? And why are some women still not allowed to vote in some parts of the world? It doesn't make sense!

A big part of gender inequality (or women being treated unequally and unfairly to men) is the mistaken idea that women aren't as capable at achieving certain things as men are, and thus should be restricted to certain inferior roles.

Here are a few quotes that paint a picture of what many men thought of women back in 1915, when the United States Congress (the law-making branch of the government) was debating whether to pass a women's suffrage law:

Women: have they a mission? Yes: It is to rule in the world of love and affection—in the home. It is not to rule in the State. They have a function to perform which precludes the latter sort of rule. Man is king of the universe; woman is queen.

—Congressman Stanley Bowdle of Ohio
  (January 12, 1915)

The Fifteenth Amendment

The Fifteenth Amendment to the US Constitution, which became official in 1870, gave Black men (but not Black women) the right to vote, stating that American citizens could not be denied the right to vote based on "race, color, or previous condition of servitude." But the Fifteenth Amendment wasn't able to fulfill its promise for almost another century. Southern states severely limited the ability of Black men to vote through tactics such as special taxes and literacy tests. A law called the Voting Rights Act was passed in 1965, which gave the majority of Black people the right to register to vote.

The Beginnings of Women's Suffrage Movements

In the nineteenth century, activists began to fight for women's suffrage. Activists are people who try to bring about social or political change through their words and actions. They did this by collecting signatures on petitions, holding rallies, making public speeches, and organizing protests. They wanted their governments to rewrite the laws so women could legally vote in both local and national elections. These activists were sometimes referred to as "suffragists." There were female as well as male suffragists.

These suffrage movements faced a lot of opposition. Many law-making politicians, and also many members of the general public, believed that women didn't deserve the same rights as men. Some suffragists were arrested. Some went on hunger strikes while in jail. Hunger strikes involve refusing to eat as a form of protest.

The women's suffrage movements in Great Britain and the United States were particularly spirited and intense.

The Start of the British Movement

In 1792, the writer and philosopher Mary Wollstonecraft (1759–1797) published the book *A Vindication of the Rights of Woman*. In the book, Wollstonecraft argued that women deserved the same rights as men—including the right to vote.

In the 1840s, the British Chartist movement took up the cause. The Chartists were working-class activists who wanted parliamentary reform. Parliament is the branch of the United Kingdom's government that is in charge of laws. It is made up of two parts, the House of Commons and the House of Lords.

The Manchester Society for Women's Suffrage formed in Manchester, England, in the mid-1860s. Its goal was to obtain the right to vote for women in national as well as local elections.

In 1867, a Member of Parliament (MP), philosopher, and economist named John Stuart Mill

presented his fellow MPs with a petition from the Manchester Society. The petition, which had approximately 1,500 signatures, demanded a law granting women the right to vote. Mill became the first MP to call for such a law. Unfortunately he was not successful with this endeavor.

Two years later, however, Parliament did pass a law allowing women taxpayers to vote in local elections. Over the next few decades, Parliament would go on to give women the right to become members of city and county councils (which are forms of local government).

Still, Parliament failed to pass a sweeping law that gave all women the right to vote in all the country's elections. Part of the reason was because the British monarch, Queen Victoria, was opposed to women's suffrage and women's rights in general, and two of the prime ministers during her reign didn't want to go against her wishes. The prime minister is the elected leader of the British government.

In 1897, the Manchester Society joined with hundreds of other suffrage societies that had formed all around the country, and together they became the National Union of Women's Suffrage Societies (NUWSS). The NUWSS was led by a suffragist named Millicent Garrett Fawcett. Despite the combined efforts of this larger and more organized group, however, Parliament still failed to pass a women's suffrage law.

Millicent Garrett Fawcett

Millicent Garrett (1847–1929) was a leader of the British women's suffrage movement for fifty years. Not only did she lead the NUWSS, she was also a founder of Newnham College in Cambridge, one of the first British colleges to admit women, and an author of multiple books and articles about women's rights.

In 1867, she married a radical politician and professor named Henry Fawcett. Millicent's older sister, Elizabeth, was also a women's rights activist. Elizabeth earned a medical degree, even though rules at the time forbid women to do so, and she went on to create a hospital for women that included an all-female staff.

In 1925, Millicent was made a Dame of the British Empire in honor of her lifelong work. (Being appointed a dame is the female version of being knighted.) A statue of her is planned for Parliament Square in London to honor her legacy. It will be the first statue of a woman to be placed there. The square currently has eleven statues of only men, including Nelson Mandela, Abraham Lincoln, and Winston Churchill.

"Deeds, Not Words"

In 1903, a British suffragist named Emmeline Pankhurst founded the Women's Social and Political Union (WSPU). Pankhurst, her daughter Christabel, and some other suffragists were frustrated by the continued failure of Parliament to grant women the right to vote. They decided that a strategy of "deeds, not words" might be more effective than the more peaceful, moderate methods of Millicent Garrett Fawcett and her organization.

The WSPU began engaging in protests that were aggressive and action-oriented. They interrupted political meetings and heckled, or shouted down, whoever was speaking. They

organized massive demonstrations and marches. They chained themselves to the iron railings outside the Parliament building and shouted, "Votes for women!"

In 1906, a British newspaper printed a story calling the WSPU suffragists "suffragettes." The "ette" ending referred to the fact that they were mostly female. It also implied that they were "small." (The suffix –ette can mean smallness, as in "kitchenette" versus "kitchen.") The WSPU didn't let this bother them; instead, they defiantly began calling themselves suffragettes too.

In 1908, the WSPU's efforts grew more extreme and sometimes violent. They vandalized mailboxes, golf courses, a famous art museum, and even the prime minister's car. Their intention was not to cause damage for the sake of causing disruption, but to draw the public's attention to the issue of women's suffrage.

BLAST BACK!

Over 1,000 suffragettes were arrested between 1908 and 1914. Emmeline and Christabel Pankhurst were among them. In prison, these suffragettes sometimes went on hunger strikes. If a protester refused to eat, the officials in charge might feel pressured into giving into his or her demands; otherwise, the protester might die of starvation. Hunger strikes were also an effective way of helping draw public attention to the cause.

In 1914, the WSPU shifted their focus to supporting the British troops during World War I, and the group would later dissolve entirely in 1917.

British Men Who
Supported Women's Suffrage

Besides John Stuart Mill, other men championed women's right to vote. They included:

Keir Hardie: an MP who attended WSPU events and worked to improve treatment of suffragettes in prison.

George Lansbury: an MP who resigned from his seat in Parliament so he could more effectively fight for suffrage. He was jailed in 1913 for making a speech at a WSPU rally.

Frederick Pethick-Lawrence: a coeditor, along with his wife, of a publication called *Votes for Women*. He too was jailed for his pro-suffrage beliefs and actions and went on a hunger strike while in prison. He became an MP in 1923 and served through 1931.

The Representation
of People Act

World War I began in 1914. On one side were
the Central Powers, which included the German
Empire, Austria-Hungary, and the Ottoman Empire
(which encompassed present-day Turkey). On the
other side were the Allies, including Great Britain,
France, Russia, and Japan. Italy and the United
States would later join the Allies.

During the war, many suffragettes turned their focus and attention to the war effort. They sent relief supplies like food and medicine to soldiers and to civilians who lived in war zones. They also raised money for the troops. Suffragettes and other women joined the workforce in huge numbers in factories, offices, and shops to fill vacancies left by the men who were away at battle.

The suffragettes' contributions raised public sympathy and support for the cause of women's suffrage, and in 1917 and 1918, Parliament passed the Representation of People Act, which finally granted women the right to vote in Great Britain.

However, this new law stated that women had to be at last thirty years old to vote. It would be another decade before women younger than thirty would be granted the same right.

One Man, One Vote

For a long time in Britain, men's suffrage was tied to income and property. Beginning in the nineteenth century, British citizens called for "one man, one vote" and demanded that Parliament grant "universal manhood suffrage"—the right for all men to vote regardless of income and property qualifications.

This was finally achieved in 1917 and 1918 with the passage of the Representation of People Act— the same law that gave women the right to vote. However, while women had to be thirty to vote, men could do so at the age of twenty-one.

Emmeline Pankhurst

Emmeline Goulden was born in Manchester, England, on July 14, 1858. In 1879, she married Richard Marsden Pankhurst, a lawyer and the author of the first woman's suffrage bill in the country. She founded the Women's Franchise League in 1889. That same year, the group won the right for married women to vote in local elections. In 1903, she founded the WSPU with her daughter Christabel.

Before World War I, Pankhurst made trips to the United States to speak about women's suffrage. The revised Representation of People Act, which lowered the voting age for women to twenty-one, was passed just a few weeks before her death on June 14, 1928.

The Beginning of the American Movement

On the other side of the Atlantic, the American movement for women's suffrage began brewing alongside the antislavery movement in the 1800s.

Until the end of the American Civil War in 1865, it was legal in some parts of the United States to keep Black people as slaves under brutal and oppressive conditions. Many activists fought to make slavery illegal; among them were Lucretia Mott and Elizabeth Cady Stanton.

Mott and Stanton came to feel that the rights of women needed to be remedied, as well as the rights of Black people. In 1848, Mott and Stanton organized a women's rights convention, or meeting, in Stanton's hometown of Seneca Falls, New York. They printed up a notice about the meeting in the local newspaper, and it took place at the Wesleyan

Methodist Chapel on July 20 and 21. At the meeting, a Declaration of Sentiments (similar to the Declaration of Independence) was created, calling for women to organize and fight for their rights, and it was signed by many suffragists. The attendees also voted to pass twelve resolutions (or stated intentions), including a resolution to fight for women's suffrage.

More conventions followed. In 1850, in Worcester, Massachusetts, a suffragist named Lucy Stone helped organize the first National Woman's Rights Convention to try to start a national suffrage movement. Over one thousand people attended. In 1852, Stanton came together with suffragist Susan B. Anthony to hold the second National Woman's Rights Convention in Syracuse, New York. Stanton and Anthony became the main leaders of the women's suffrage movement for the next half-century. There were many other conventions too, and over time, the momentum for women's suffrage grew stronger.

Susan B. Anthony

Susan Brownell Anthony was born in Adams, Massachusetts, on February 15, 1820. She was an activist in the temperance (or anti-alcohol) and antislavery movements. After the passage of the Fifteenth Amendment that gave Black men the right to vote, she turned her attention to women's suffrage.

Along with Elizabeth Cady Stanton, she founded the National Woman Suffrage Association in 1869. In 1872, Anthony voted in the presidential election, even though she didn't have a legal right to do so. Once her crime was discovered, she was tried and ordered to pay a fine of $100, but she refused, saying "Taxation without representation is tyranny."

In 1890, she became the president of the National American Woman Suffrage Association (which was an evolution of the National Woman Suffrage Association). Sadly, she died in 1906 before women's suffrage became a reality in the United States.

Elizabeth Cady Stanton

Elizabeth Cady was born in Johnstown, New York, on November 12, 1815. After graduating from Emma Willard's Troy Female Seminary in Troy, New York, she studied law in the office of her father, a US congressman. There, she learned firsthand about laws that discriminated against women, and she decided to commit herself to the fight for gender equality.

In 1840, she married Henry Brewster Stanton, who was a lawyer and antislavery activist. In June of that year, they attended the World's Antislavery Convention in London, where she, Lucretia Mott, and other women were not allowed to participate. This outraged Stanton and fueled her commitment to women's rights. She helped pass an 1848 law in the state of New York that gave married women property rights.

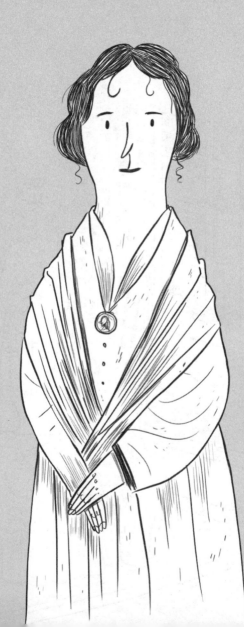

Stanton and Susan B. Anthony worked together closely for fifty years after the first National Woman's Rights Convention in Seneca Falls. They planned campaigns, gave speeches, wrote letters and pamphlets, and championed changes to the laws to make sure women received equal treatment. Stanton died in New York City on October 26, 1902.

The National Woman's Party

In 1913, American suffragists Alice Paul and Lucy Burns formed a women's rights group called the Congressional Union for Woman Suffrage. Paul and Burns had been involved in the British suffrage movement. In 1916, the group was renamed the National Woman's Party (NWP).

The NWP used militant tactics to fight for suffrage, similar to the WSPU in Britain. Among other things, NWP members were the firest to picket the White House and conducted other acts of civil disobedience. Many members were arrested and jailed, and some went on hunger strikes while in prison.

MR. PRESIDENT WHAT WILL YOU DO FOR WOMAN SUFFRAGE

Other Suffragists

There were many other important figures in the American and British women's suffrage movements. Here are just a few:

Sojourner Truth: The daughter of slaves, she was a social activist and evangelist who fought for the rights of Black women and men.

Julia Ward Howe: Howe was an American suffragist and the author of the lyrics to "Battle Hymn of the Republic," which she wrote during the Civil War to the tune of an old folk song.

Alice Stone Blackwell: The daughter of suffragist Lucy Stone, she was the editor of *Woman's Journal*, a leading women's rights newspaper in the United States.

Carrie Chapman Catt: Catt was an American feminist leader and president of the National American Woman Suffrage Association after Susan B. Anthony.

Mary Church Terrell: The daughter of slaves, she was a social activist and member of the National American Woman Suffrage Association. She advocated for the rights of Black women.

Helen Taylor: The stepdaughter of suffragist John Stuart Mill and daughter of suffragist Harriet Taylor Mill, she worked for women's rights.

Emily Davison: In what many consider to be an act of protest against the British government for not granting women's suffrage, Davison walked onto a racetrack during the Epsom Derby horse race and stepped in front of the king's charging horse. She died four days later.

Mary Richardson: A Canadian who joined the British suffrage movement, she was famous for slashing a valuable painting by Spanish painter Diego Velásquez in the National Gallery museum in London as an act of protest.

The Nineteenth Amendment

American women did have some voting rights. For example, the territory of Wyoming (which would not become a state until 1890) gave women the right to vote in all elections in 1869.

But the only way to make sure all American women could vote in all elections was to pass an amendment to the federal Constitution.

Elizabeth Cady Stanton and Susan B. Anthony founded the National Woman Suffrage Association in 1869 with the express purpose of seeing such an amendment passed. That same year, Lucy Stone founded another group called the American Woman Suffrage Association. In 1890, the two organizations joined together and called themselves the National American Woman Suffrage Association.

During the end of the nineteenth century and the beginning of the twentieth, the momentum for women's suffrage grew. After Wyoming passed their women's suffrage law, there was more and more pressure on other states to pass similar laws. By 1915,

women had the same voting rights as men in eleven states. And since women could now vote in these states, they could elect government officials who supported women's rights—including suffrage.

But there was still no constitutional amendment to guarantee all American women the right to vote. Two versions of the amendment had gone before Congress in 1878 and 1914, but neither resolution had been passed.

Finally, in 1918 and 1919, the amendment was voted into law by Congress. The amendment became official when it was ratified, or approved, by all the states in 1920.

However, the ratification passed by only one vote. A young lawmaker from Tennessee, Harry Burn, changed his vote at the last minute from no to yes after receiving a letter from his mother telling him to do so. Later, he explained, "I know that a mother's advice is always safest for her boy to follow."

This Nineteenth Amendment to the Constitution stated:

> The right of citizens of the United States to vote shall not be denied or abridged by the United States or by any State on account of sex.

What About Native Americans?

Even after the passage of the Nineteenth Amendment, Native American women and men could not vote in national elections for another four years. And some states refused to grant Native American women that right for even longer.

The Equality State

Wyoming, which was the first American state to give full voting rights to women, also happened to be the first state to elect a woman for governor. Nellie Tayloe Ross was elected governor in 1924 and served in that office until 1927. In 1933, she became the first woman director of the US Mint, which produces all the coins that are in use in the United States.

Wyoming's official nickname is the Equality State.

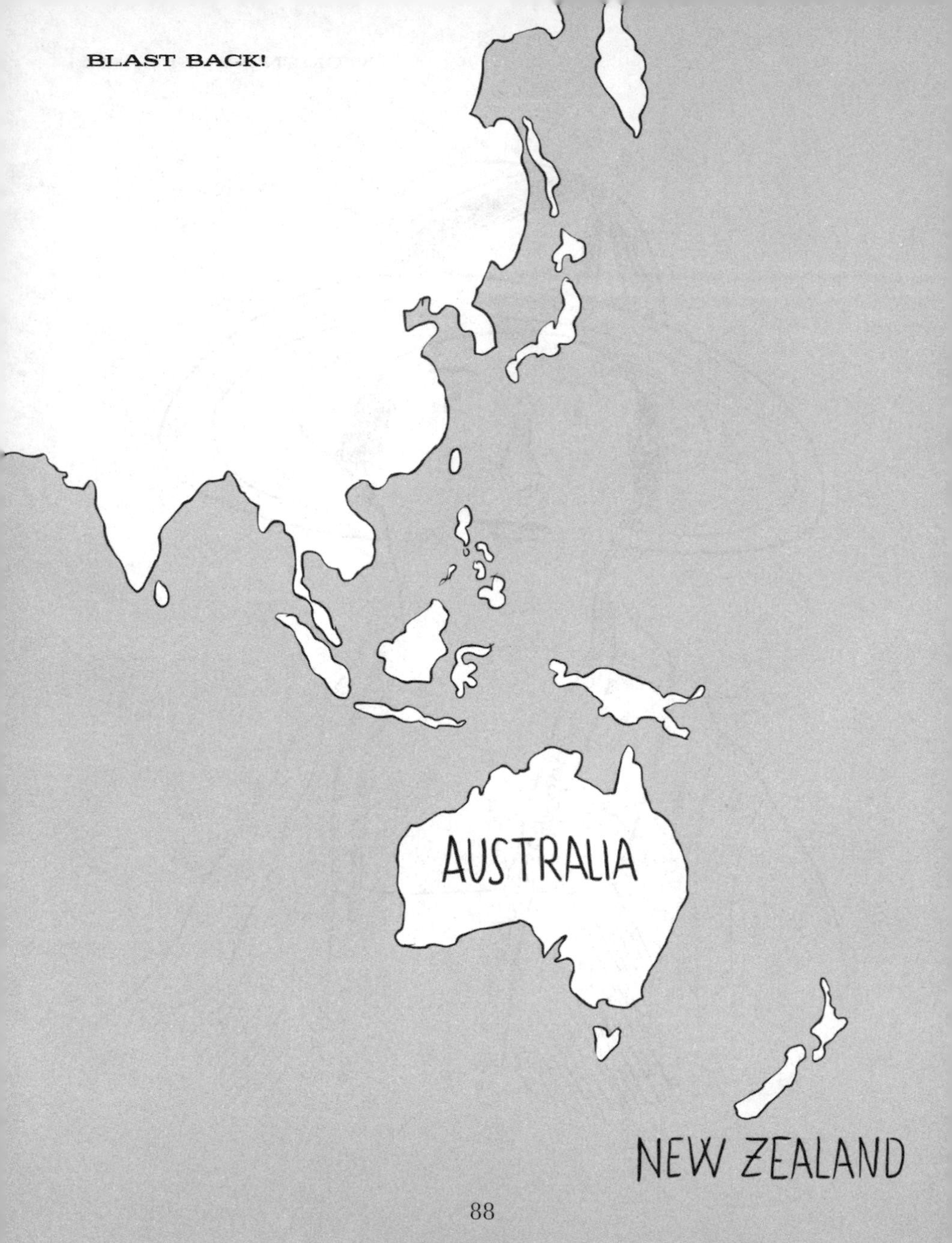

AUSTRALIA

NEW ZEALAND

The First Countries to Support Women's Suffrage

The United States and Britain weren't the first to pass women's suffrage laws. In 1893, New Zealand became the first country to grant all women, even Maori women, the right to vote. In 1902, Australia became the second, although aboriginal women and men were excluded until 1962.

Other countries passed women's suffrage laws before or around the same time the United States and Britain passed theirs, including:

Canada, 1918
(First Nations were not granted the right to vote until 1960)

Finland, 1906

Norway, 1913

Soviet Russia, 1917

Poland, 1918

Czechoslovakia, 1919

Germany, 1918

Austria, 1918

Hungary, 1920

American Men Who Supported Women's Suffrage

The American women's suffrage movement had many male supporters. James Mott, Lucretia Mott's husband, presided over the Seneca Falls convention of 1848. Frederick Douglass was at the convention as well. A total of thirty-two men signed the Declaration of Sentiments at the convention.

Men were involved in various women's suffrage groups, including the American Woman Suffrage Association and the National American Woman Suffrage Association. Starting around 1910, men began forming their own groups in support of women's suffrage, such as the national Men's League for Women's Suffrage, which boasted 20,000 members in 1912.

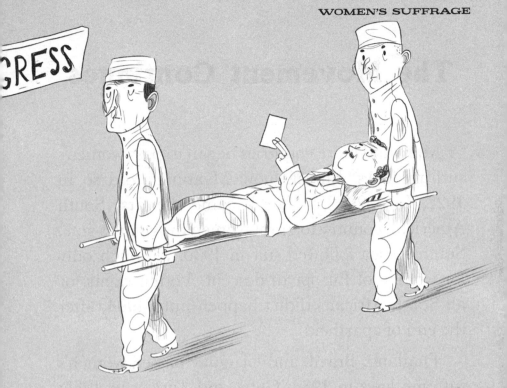

When the crucial vote for the Nineteenth Amendment took place in Congress, some Congressmen went to heroic efforts to cast a yes vote. One congressman was unable to walk, so he was carried in on a stretcher so he could vote. Another had broken his shoulder, but put off treatment so he could vote. Still another congressman left his wife's deathbed to vote.

The Movement Continues

More and more countries began to pass women's suffrage laws. Burma (now Myanmar) did so in 1922. In 1929, Ecuador became the first South American country to grant women the right to vote. South Africa followed suit in 1930, although only for women of European descent. Voting rights for all South Africans didn't happen until 1994, after the end of apartheid.

Thailand, Brazil, and Uruguay passed women's suffrage laws in 1932; Cuba and Turkey in 1934; and the Philippines in 1937.

After World War II ended in 1945, China, Japan, Romania, Italy, France, and Yugoslavia passed women's suffrage laws. India and Pakistan did so after they gained independence from Great Britain in 1947.

Over the next two decades, the total number of countries with women's suffrage laws climbed to over one hundred. In 1973, Syrian women gained the right to vote. In the 1970s, only a few European countries, including Portugal, Spain, Moldova, and Switzerland, still didn't allow women to vote, although that would change by the end of the century.

The Convention on the Political Rights of Women

In March 1953, the United Nations adopted a document called the "Convention on the Political Rights of Women." The purpose of the document was to establish basic political rights for women around the world.

The document states: "Women shall be entitled to vote in elections on equal terms with men, without any discrimination."

Women's Suffrage in the Twenty-First Century

By 2005, Saudi Arabia was the only place in the world besides Vatican City that did not have a women's suffrage law. (Vatican City, the smallest country in the world, is a country within the city of Rome.) This changed in 2011 when King Abdullah of Saudi Arabia granted women the right to vote and run for local elections starting with the 2015 election. But even to this day, it is not easy for Saudi women to vote. Among other things, strict laws forbid women from driving, whether to the polls or anywhere else.

Vatican City remains the only country where women can't vote.

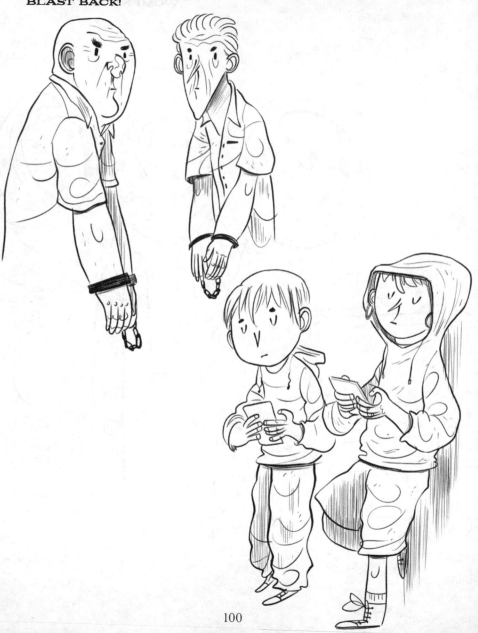

People Who Can't Vote

Besides women in Vatican City, there are other categories of people who are not permitted to vote. For example, in the United States, felons (criminals who have been convicted of a felony-class offense), those who are considered mentally incompetent (which means that a court of law has declared that person incapable of making rational decisions due to mental illness or another factor), and those under eighteen years of age can't legally vote.

The Legacy of Women's Suffrage

Much has changed in the last century and a half for women's suffrage. Except for Vatican City, women around the world can uniformly vote and run for political office.

But gender inequality remains a problem. In 2017, there were only fifteen female world leaders. The United States has never had a female president. Men far outnumber women in lower political offices too.

Additionally, while women have the right to vote, they (along with other groups like the economically vulnerable) don't always have the means to. This includes having access to transportation, adequate childcare, time off from work, and whatever else is necessary to get to the polls and exercise their legal right to vote.

Activists are still fighting to make sure that women and men are guaranteed equal rights and that women and men of color are also guaranteed equal rights with white women and men.

On January 21, 2017, the day after Donald Trump took office as president of the United States, millions of women and men gathered all over the

world to march in protest against his exclusionary views and policies. Like the brave individuals a century before them who had marched for suffrage in America, Britain, and elsewhere, they marched in solidarity for women's rights, civil rights, and human rights. As long as there is gender inequality and other kinds of inequality, people all over will continue to come together to champion justice.

Well, it's been a great adventure. Goodbye, women's suffrage!

Where to next?

Also available:

Selected Bibliography

63 Congressional Record. Session 3. Volume 52. 1915.

Britannica Kids. kids.britannica.com.

Cohen, Jennie. "The Mother Who Saved Suffrage: Passing the Nineteenth Amendment." *History*. August 16, 2010. http://www.history.com/news/the-mother-who-saved-suffrage-passing-the-19th-amendment.

"Elizabeth Garrett Anderson." *BBC*. 2014. http://www.bbc.co.uk/history/historic_figures/garrett_anderson_elizabeth.shtml.

Encyclopedia Britannica. www.britannica.com.

Erlanger, Steven. "Millicent Fawcett is First Woman to Get Statue in London's Parliament Square." *New York Times*. April 2, 2017. https://www.nytimes.com/2017/04/02/world/europe/millicent-fawcett-statue-london.html.

"Frederick Douglass." *National Park Service*. February 26, 2015. https://www.nps.gov/wori/learn/historyculture/frederick-douglass.htm.

Geiger, Abigail, and Lauren Kent. "Number of Women Leaders around the World Has Grown, But They're Still a Small Group." *Pew Research Center*. March 8, 2017. http://www.pewresearch.org/fact-tank/2017/03/08/women-leaders-around-the-world.

"Male Supporters of Women's Suffrage." *Parliament*. http://www.parliament.uk/about/living-heritage/transformingsociety/electionsvoting/womenvote/overview/male-sympathisers.

"The Manchester Society for Women's Suffrage." *The National Archives*. http://discovery.nationalarchives.gov.uk/details/r/604bfcb0-97a1-4dd9-899c-25b7564642d0.

"Men Support the Woman Suffrage Movement." *National Women's History Museum*. 2007. https://www.nwhm.org/online-exhibits/rightsforwomen/menforsuffrage.html.

Perlman, Merrill. "Shades of Suffrage: -ette vs. -is." *Columbia Journalism Review*. July 22, 2015. https://www.cjr.org/analysis/shades_of_suffrage_-ette_vs_-ist.php.

Przybyla, Heidi M., and Fredreka Schouten. "At 2.6 Million Strong, Women's Marches Crush Expectations." *USA Today*. January 21, 2017. https://www.usatoday.com/story/news/politics/2017/01/21/womens-march-aims-start-movement-trump-inauguration/96864158.

"Women Who Fought for the Vote." *History*. 2009. http://www.history.com/topics/womens-history/women-who-fought-for-the-vote.

NANCY OHLIN is the author of the YA novels *Always, Forever* and *Beauty* as well as the early chapter book series Greetings from Somewhere under the pseudonym Harper Paris. She lives in Ithaca, New York, with her husband, their two kids, four cats, and assorted animals who happen to show up at their door. Visit her online at nancyohlin.com.

ROGER SIMÓ is an illustrator based in a town near Barcelona, where he lives with his wife, son, and daughter. He has become the person that he would have envied when he was a child: someone who makes a living by drawing and explaining fantastic stories.